Mercies in the American Desert

poems

Mercies in the American Desert

Benjamin Landry

Louisiana State University Press
Baton Rouge

Published by Louisiana State University Press
www.lsupress.org

LSU Press Paperback Original

Designer: Barbara Neely Bourgoyne
Typeface: Adobe Caslon

Cover photograph: Untitled, 2012, by Bernadette Witzack

Library of Congress Cataloging-in-Publication Data
Names: Landry, Benjamin, author.
Title: Mercies in the American desert : poems / Benjamin Landry.
Description: Baton Rouge : Louisiana State University Press, [2021]
Identifiers: LCCN 2020028318 (print) | LCCN 2020028319 (ebook) | ISBN
    978-0-8071-7311-4 (paperback) | ISBN 978-0-8071-7519-4 (pdf) | ISBN
    978-0-8071-7520-0 (epub)
Subjects: LCGFT: Poetry.
Classification: LCC PS3612.A5487 M47 2021 (print) | LCC PS3612.A5487 (ebook) |
    DDC 811/.6—dc23
LC record available at https://lccn.loc.gov/2020028318
LC ebook record available at https://lccn.loc.gov/2020028319

This collection is especially for Iris.

[. . . T]he Christians who were driven into the American Desart, which is now called New England, have to their sorrow seen Azazel dwelling and raging there in very Tragical Instances.

—Cotton Mather, "The History of New-England," *Magnalia Christi Americana*

Nothing exists by itself.
The moonlight seemed to.

  —Wallace Stevens, "Les Plus Belles Pages"

CONTENTS

Mercies in the American Desert

Satellite

We are being watched by . . .
We have lost communication with . . .

[. . . technically, anything orbiting].

All our names for them were
                                    auspicious;
It was circumstances that didn't
        live up.

And so,   phosphorescent
        ejaculation,
                    angelic
                    castoff,

robot drudge
        with solar-powered
                    foresight.

With each pass,
        you tell
us we are
                    beautiful,

                            and we
are starting
        to believe you,

the snow
        on the screen

ourselves,
our smithereens.

I

Meep Meep

This against a backdrop by O'Keeffe: desert skulls picked clean,
flowers like vaginas crowding out the cacti, sexing back the sun.

How we run on and on, how we take turns painting tunnels
into rock faces, going through, then effacing them.

We're Bonnie-and-Clyde, bundling TNT. We're the sort
who scoff at tall glasses of water. Instead, we drink sand:

our delusions sustain us as we speed down the unmarked highway
toward an improvised vanishing point. We never get entirely away.

Our backpacks are stuffed with silver parachutes of grief.
When we come to a cliff, we leap, or we saw off our own

pinnacles by hand. The BNSF loops past us in the morning
when we wake, your flightless feathers curled usefully over my snout.

It will end the way it began. Sometimes your love straps rockets
to his old-timey roller skates and you, you just have to let him go.

Espalier

n. A row of trees so trained
that the rioting of Eden
was hemmed in

and birds, arrested
on the wing, were re-arrayed
on wires, on limbs.

It was all so instantly formulaic
to even the untrained animal brain.
The lion stopped playing

tiddlywinks with the lamb
and—obeying the new paradigm—ate it.
Rivers felt their banks for the first time.

The waste upon which the gate
opened up was the rest of their lives.
They were its equal.

When the mynah bird gave up its mantra
at that long day's end, She found His ear
and whispered, "Give me that pain again."

Scuttling

It has to do with turnout.

Gray scuttling at the edge of vision.

What seemed like spirits
    were
mice among the Duracells.

In just that way,
within the city's rigorous
        geometries,
we stayed wild,

    dusted
bodies made to slip
  in and out
of moments, light, even
       cracks
within light.

Thirst, a certain
necessity
   of touch,
a certain
  obsessiveness
of language,

going deaf,
    filthy
and miraculous.

Pina

I saw Pina Bausch heron dancing down the grassy median of a tree-lined boulevard. She wore a blue shirt, black pants, and was otherwise unchanged by death. As she went, she brushed her chest with her flight feathers. Then, she seemed to preen and roost in the high branches of an evergreen. I knew—as one sometimes does when dreaming—that I had brought her into being, that she was in some way part of me, so what explained my difficulty in keeping up? Her blurring at the edges, *in extremis?* All I know is I have seen the heron move this way a handful of times. Gathering, gathering itself and then stooping into flight.

Undergrowth

To be moral, pretty and sparse,
where a telling thread of clothing
caught. Some magpie amasses
his candy foils. Fire springs
up there like an idea suddenly
occurring to the wilderness.

Often, a human form, down
on all fours. A rabbit warren,
eyes all pupil gazing at the moon.
Or some bush-tailed predator
watching for that glint of watching.

Bunyan

The pines make themselves a fire,
and it is my job to face away
and say, "Keep your distance.
Come no closer than the length of an ax."
The light feels strange on my neck,
fire merely the sprouting sensation
between my shoulder blades.
Don't worry, I am not so hirsute,
nor am I angelic. My rheumatoid knuckles
wrapped in a dirty kerchief.
In a forest like this, you misplace
your swagger. The screech
of the screech owl cuts you down
at the knees. I have forgotten
the sense of flesh, its heft, have
lost my feel for the grain of it.
I am the tender, the tinder,
the tenderer. No wonder
the beasts ignore me now.

Hydrangeas

Now that they have lost their bonnets of snow,
they turn their baffled heads to the camera:

What's my motivation?

You should've seen them last September
when they were sunset pink. But the dead
have the habit of sticking around, spilling
out of the diners to vote conservative.

Thank goodness the kids are in school
and beyond convincing. They are unsentimental
about the monster-headed flower and cut switches
and take turns rapping one another on the thighs
as it has been done for autumns immemorial.

Old Marble Vast

do not touch down
my medusa
jellyfish   like
something I have
known once
grown deadly

I was always
at the edge
of frame   witness
rather than subject
and you made
the blue distance
first bearable
then intelligible
an interstitial
balm

      too near
to you and I
lose focus
too close
and I forfeit
my skin

For Those Who Would Squander Love, the Earthworm Has Five Hearts

Sometimes your language is unbecoming.
Sometimes you are in no mood.
Today is just such a day, trees
with their branches bent and broken
under the weight of their fruit.

Private Booth

It's disturbing to recall
the child's analogy of adult desire:

how you were certain to be
in parlor view

of your grandmother's cuckoo clock
moments before the hour.

That's the suggestive silence
of all the engines at rest,

every toggle switch
in the OFF position,

the warehouse
of robotic arms recumbent.

If you've a mind for irony,
think of it as any dovecote,

the drowse inside
as thick as feathers,

the brooding of the cubbies
like the winter-muffle of an empty cauldron.

All that changes
with the final *chink*

of two dollars
in widely circulated coins.

The deliciousness of that silence
set to brass lights,

then trance music
picking up a slow grind,

hackles stirring
beyond smoked glass.

A body, choreographed,
ruffles its feathers,

sets the fittings taut before
stepping into the time allotted.

Museum on Fire

The forty-year-old
caught on Oxy
reaches for his wallet
like a museum on fire.

Later, when his parents bury him,
they become unable to speak
his name and are, themselves,
a museum on fire.

When we sang Mémère
"Happy Birthday,"
she could not recognize us
and instead wore the absent look
of a museum on fire.

This last decade, when so little
and still so much happened,
I often caught it passing quickly
in a mirror:
a museum on fire.

When the White House deleted
climate change research,
that was a museum on fire.

Sometimes, love is patient,
love is kind. But sometimes
it is a museum on fire.

African Grey

Listening to the wind when you
have gone is like having
an African Grey to keep me ghostly
company, who at night speaks
from under a shroud in the kitchen
corner in your voice.

One picks up constantly after
the departed. They, too, require
food and water. One's shoulder smarts
from where they, habitually, stand.

I try to move carefully, now, as though
to avoid your good-natured rebuke
that something as simple as opening
a bag could've been handled
with a little more grace.

Still Life

Wheeled to the window
to blush at the folly of dawn.
Maybe love is the afternoon
of poised barroom darts,
the empty threat
of a green cloud
with no mountain
to break itself against.

—To crack open the vista
and pour out all the birdsong
into my Twenty-First Century
hearing horn! But you
will look at your hands and say
Give him what he wants now
and when will it end?

Slippers and Underthings

A lax rendering or lull. She was wronged
but now drives long-haul freight to those
rough stations so ill-equipped to receive it.

♦

We are ill-equipped to receive
those children who leave home hungry,
school the least of their worries.

♦

School the least of their worries
into a persistent weather pattern
which psychologists are calling Seasonal
Affective Disorder: sun just nicking above horizon.
It can be difficult to get out of bed.

♦

It can be difficult to get out of bed,
that delicious smother of down.
First the night paints our eyes bronze;
then the morning comes back with white lead.

Shaft of Light

perhaps

   stammers the

perhaps
       hand

perhaps brow

    of swimmer

that is

     chevrons

       of forearm

and thigh

    and a few

   bathing
       digital moths

late arrived

    that could

be fire-colored

or set

   afire

how

    they grapple

toward

    the present

understanding
      or threaten

    to disperse

Mercies in the American Desart

for Sara

i

Say we have not seen rain
in so many months.

Deep in the woods,
there is a tire half sunk in weeds

with enough spring melt in the well
to fill the hemlocks with mosquito-drone.

ii

I was correcting papers on the back porch
and simultaneously turning over

the folly of naming an unborn child. A fox,
meanwhile, crept out to preen on Discovery Rock.

Maybe he was actually lame in one forepaw.
Maybe he was playing for sympathy.

iii

When we came in from the terrible wilds
of not knowing each other,

you told me to keep my voice down
and laughed at my clumsiness.

Then, you reached to help me
with the clasp.

II

[Darling]

The function of the manta ray
is to swallow darkness,
its ghostface intelligent
if uncomprehending in a way
that speaks to our condition.

We have had enough of volition.
We want air without reason.

Say *breathe*

          and the cage expands,
taking the dimensions of the lung
      with it.

        Heel-to-toe,
measure the inside of this temporary room,

the wingspan of the ray,
      mid-contraction,
           held in the ocean's updraft.

Say *breathe out*

         the cage collapses
[words to reassure].

Recess

salt the walkway

and crystal

one's understanding

there are

cleavages in language

the brine

seeps up the mineral bath

what

soothes the cut

and we've kept

our heads down

on our desks too long

hoping it would

stop happening

on its own

maybe it takes

fracture

earth giving way

one

is apprehended

in stone

always that compulsion

to put

a tongue

to stone

if only because it tastes

of another

shore

another

time

we become

porous with time

decades

in the fine bones

of the feet
                    I want to discover
more than that
                    I want
    to be found

Ear Worm

So sue me if the song won't end.
It's in the public domain,
and its primary stipulation is that we
have to dance or pretend we have
somewhere we need to be, which is fine
until, overheard: "I've had quite enough
of them voweling around in bed
like the Old Masters." And we're

banished to the kitchen. I'm never sure
how many wedges a cake should be
cut into, are you? Better overserve, nay?
But then, I'm not the sort who expects
anyone to be capable of eating
however much cake: any amount
is a charming surprise. What changed
me meaningfully and forever was

the bristly pines, how their birds
seemed put-upon, their songs strung
like garlands around the orange waists.
How in their long, dark indeterminacy,
even the most realistic of them
seemed painted by Impressionists,
how they looked down their endless
muzzles like thoroughbreds or Narcissi

down the tragic, protracted history
of their self-regard.

She Asked Me to Explain

SB

Do you know the helix,
amino acids only meaning
something in combination?

Or the wasp, how it papers
over the queen?

I want to give you what
you want, a simple truth
to carry around in a manila folder,

but the image keeps intruding
on the verb, and pretty
soon, it is too gold-limned
and gorgeous to make
sense of, to make speak
plain English, this thing
that lies down with you
at the edge of perception.

I never thought I would see
the mountain mask and subtract
itself from new light, but there it is.

Where Once

little nameless
flowers
—and lo—
unring me

not even
a stump
where once
a tree

one does not
see   one
feels the logic
of it plain

must be
long-rotten roots
gone to earth
like all
thoughts buried
but like the tree
the poem

implausibly
here

Stock Ponds

like pools of mercury in Ohio.
When you live in a land so platter-flat,
you feel like the head of St. John the Baptist.

I couldn't find a job. We went
to the beach in Lorain and decided
against. That was the summer

they shot Tamir Rice and then even
the produce sections of grocery stores
felt defeated, despite all the apparent
abundance. The misters couldn't keep up.
It wasn't always that way. It was once

the blessed floor of a prehistoric ocean.
You and I would've been dinosaurs
with long paddle appendages instead
of newcomers looking for a clean
swimming hole, searching out
a windbreak, a tree farm, anything.

Surely You Jest

I was about to say a tunnel of white oaks
and concord grape vines. I'll call the town
if anyone tries to cut it back, let in more sunlight.
Foxes wouldn't know what to do with it.
Crows would have to call off searching
for their upside down Nixon, the poor
graduate researchers. And deer wouldn't
come round here anymore. So, preserve
the man on his back. Let the edifice of clouds
rush by, the wet mouth and the too-green
clover in May, still without their ivory
or purple pom-poms. There was once
a neighbor with hysterical pregnancy
in his wife's satin dressing gown. That story
and many others and houses with which
the rushing river absconds. I know,
you're trying to have a serious conversation,
but it is reunion weekend and every maple
you approach has initials carved in skin.

Aquarium

Ours the epitome of functional neglect,
all algae and suckerfish draped
from the glass like brocaded Renaissance
sleeves. Snails are the roaches of this
Apocalypse, pulverized stones beneath
their sensitive feet. They seem
to reach for language, and the suckerfish
are the brooding gods of their cosmos.
It goes on inexorably: in just this way,
we developed lungs and beautiful
speaking voices and a sense that we
—pressing our faces to the glass—
were being shortchanged.

Sing

they're babes
                haven't heard
Billie Holiday   sing strange fruit
                danger is
learning patriotism before shame
                              lyric
before melody
            hand on heart

prisons   are filled
            those stars
are skittish
          tumbling   those stars
are falling
                  say it with me   out
of the night
    out of the flag

   a white kid
from the suburbs   you'll say
how could he   you'll say

      I don't know

when   I first heard
      Billie Holiday
              sing
strange fruit

        my father
           taught
history
    I don't know

I'll confess
    I don't know
when I first heard

       somehow
I knew   it happened
              was and is happening
      all the while

Black Banks

Like a nudibranch
giving onto a tenant farm.

We ourselves arrived by ferry—
emerald in that red clay land.

I would make the crossing
many times in subsequent years
outside of waking hours.

It was almost indecent,
how it chipped and scalloped
and made our living in relief.

Stone was a factor,
but by no means the only,
nor the most important one.

The trees counted for something,
more or less vertical, regimented,
windswept as brushes of baleen.

Farm machinery
rusted fast here and there
in fields that refused passage
today, as though
after much deliberation

they were sticking
with their ochres and the dust
and the sea spray they swore by.

Dream of *Zenyatta* Dancing

In a moment
[Important to avoid]

A stuttering
kick-step. [the dead

language] *of delirious*
boredom In the paddock

[of 'never'] before start time,
[and 'always.'] the trainer kept

firebugs the filly's mouth
[Why so easy to speak]

drove down
wet with a sponge.

[against the body,]
She appeared

[its specific]
to be trying to say

to the grocery store
[eloquence?] and say

against *its slumbering*
artificial the *turf.*

bit
How perfectly

the first fruit
and the leading hand.

fell On the oval,
even the bruising

she stamped
picturesque

They set it
with joy *ablaze.*

Clean Slate

The problem is the infrastructure of dreaming has fallen
on hard times. We want nothing so much as

the promise of Yucca Mountain, a sweating red
heart beating deep underground. For this, we stockpile

dynamite, jackhammers. We buy new hardhats
for the ribbon cutting. We show up on the appointed

morning, but there are no photographers and no orange
coolers of ice water; we've been sold a scale model,

just a rectangular plot of packed earth. The sun is a steady
acetylene torch. It's clear we each must dig and so

roll the sleeves of our dress shirts in unison past
our elbows. Though we're disappointed, it feels good

to swing a pickaxe, harpoon the ground with a shovel.
In the dullness of the work, we can almost imagine

the famed hanging gardens saturated with flowers.

Time of Asters

It used to come so naturally;
now, we wait to have a human feeling.

Duck, duck, duck and cover.

The new poll numbers are said
to lull and dazzle.

I won't read them, I swear.

In the time of asters, I won't be
distracted from their orange hubs,
their blueflame spokes.

All around is rising water and rust.

The dead awake to the dream
of our livid and living blue.

Idyll

Imported sand shimmers best and holds, holds the impression of palm. The good saucer is for scalloping out the burrows, little graves for plastic men. A call somewhere? No, a creeper drumming on a birch. I keep my arm still and birchlike, wanting drumming. Safety glass broken and hand like a minor scald. All winter the maple wept into a plastic jug, now only healing bark and spigot good for the taste of metal on the tongue. Blood. Brother, come no closer. I will invent a special winter for you with none of the berries you like that split into threes. My dozer keeps one eye open: it only seems to doze. A curtain. Mother is watching while scalping a colander of strawberries. She does this for us. I will tell her I want my tooth back and would gladly give any amount of money. And that windmill? Levering itself off the ground, glint, landing with a *clump?* Lever, glint, *clump?* That is Father.

At the Mouth of the St. Lawrence

c. 1640

—Their expressions where they stood
on the rocky shore as the first bright
orange washed up. They would've moved
the pelts from their faces, red regions
mapped on their necks from a season of gnats,
licked their lips white with tallow.

Maybe they'd dreamt something like this
at the last killing moon, their lean-tos
battened under snow. Or recalled
the carts piled high on market days
in the village of Hanc, which is how
they knew a word for it out of this

rough cut. There would've been
a child in water up to his knees reaching
for the fruit, a flame. From the far bank,
shadows of spruces like tall flints.

From Atlanta

for Juanita Harper

She said what struck
her most was the lack
of streetlamps
in Connecticut.

Her son—before
he died—played
a mean game
of bb gun
one-pump,
each boy
his own team.

Longing and defiant
pointing at other boys,
muzzle-hearted
in the great stillness
that was our field
before everyone's pops
came home. Years

later, Julian picked
the back of his neck
and a long-lodged
bb came rattling
out, blue-black
and scarlet

like the planet Mars
you could only see
in Connecticut,
Darkness like you
wouldn't believe.

Night Vision

for Paul

He chose the darkest part for us
between the campsite and communal fire.
Said this was just the place to teach us

night vision, which he'd perfected
as a Reservist in the jungles
of Florida, a simulated drop

behind enemy lines in Nam,
where survival depended on following
the footfalls of shy, nocturnal beasts.

Or picking out the metal catch
of a mine in the shuddering moonlight—
which, in these New England woods,

he translated into spreading roots
—splayed—tendons of hands—
across the paths. The sniper's mark

was a spinner's web at temple level.
Our task was to set our sight
on the sightless part,

then wait for the pupils' dilation,
trusting the way to reveal itself
out of the barked periphery.

For some time, we stumbled—
horses riding into blinders.
The path we pretended to see

was only his voice, which we followed
through red oaks, scuffing
our boots on swaybacked stones.

When it happened, it was exactly
like looking through a stereogram,
the snow-white static of this

perceived world falling away,
the trails of badger and deer,
litter-drag of porcupines, the retreat

made implicit to the un-learned eye.
Years later, I'm at the sudden funeral
of his wife. He wears his grief

like a new shirt, self-consciously,
and I suppose there isn't any other way.
I'm one of the scrupulous mourners

who wait for him to cross the mortuary lot.
That is when I notice
his slant-faced approach.

He is not-looking for the way,
trying night vision in broad day. I watch
him watch the static fall away.

That Other Life

A leak develops in the front-end exhaust; my best friend's
mother fell asleep forever this way. I dismiss the idea of
God, but not that other life like an inarticulate shade
stretched across the lawn, a figure behind laundry pinned
up or taken down. Not after. Concomitant. A huntsman
spider crawls to me with its wide embrace. We are neither
of us afraid. His eight images make a perfect, composite
sense. Could I not imagine a ninth? Beauty is a comfort,
but it is not the same as being beheld.

III

Left in Charge of the Garden

I don't know what to do
with roses once they go.
I suppose I should read up,
but I like overseeing the denouement
almost as much as the flowering.
If there are a few late petals
holding on, it's okay to tousle
them like the head of a child.

When the ants catch wind
of this disintegration, they
are jealous, come methodically
running. And I wonder if
their lairs are lined with pink
rose petals like some Victoria's
Secret grotto, or if they are making
rosewater with their bodies'
enzymes for the queen. Perhaps

this is how roses factor into being
useful, not merely the failed
vocabulary of experiment, the thing
saved between pages or else
pinned to the breast, a dead
idea. Rose in the morning.
Rose from the mourning. Rose
in unison from our open mouths.

At a Remove

Say it's on principle,
for art. To make
of one's arms an X,
a technique
of shirt removal.

A strong gust
of the west
precipitates
the thwacks
of broom handles
in garbage-scented
alleys and on
wraparound
porches across
this great
bread basket.

I prefer
the false mountain,
the one comprised
of snakes of color
moving
in the water.

I'd live there
if I could,
instead of
this pile
of failed silos
we've set afire.

We should run,
but we like
the heat painting
our faces.
Later, it will hurt
to smile, but we
won't be smiling,
exactly, as we do

what we do
to each other
in the field
of soybeans

while a kite turns
above us to see
if we are animal,
and if so, how spry
or badly wounded.

Unlearning Object Permanence

Appearance, disappearance
make the hidden logic
visible.

Start with a coin, an orange.
A woman goes
behind a tree. A man
goes behind the ground.

An explosion of starlings
upends the solid,
classical architecture.

Ruin is the new sublime:
trillium at the salt flats.

Shelter

worms' drillwork
        is a beam

blood knocking
        a valve

eel's dream
        is a horse's sinus

prayer don't come slouching
back this mouth doesn't want you

in *Jurassic Park* the children
        make a roof out of Plexiglas
and their own extremities
        Tyrannosaurus is the weather

we've each in turn
        been put out (and I
    don't mean 'inconvenienced')

see how the paint fades

I cannot walk in the forest
        anymore each trunk
has come to seem load bearing
the angels
        so very heavy and threatening

Lineage

someone mentions 'tenderest'
you want to believe
superlatives mean
nothing to you

if your wife
werent always
saying 'always'
and your doctor
werent likewise
always saying 'never'

the daisy
on the other hand
is charmingly
indeterminate
part weed
part aster

if only you might
enjoy the subtleties
instead of forcing
language to its knees
or better yet

walking it to a cliff
as though you were merely
being solicitous
Good Mother Tongue
Good Father Death

cant you see
language is trembling
cant you see
it just wants down

Gina Haspel and the Honey Bee

someone decided torture was a good idea

                                              trying to warm up by the heat
                                                       of a flower

and then someone decided

                                              the bees on neonicotinoid

someone decided to make tapes
of the torture

                                        bees drowning on information
                                                  pollen-bemused

and then when the public

                                                  stamen-struck

came round to its senses
destroy the tapes

                                                losing track of time
                                              lashed to the sepal

for years   no one
was held to account

                                        the temperature dropped

as though the incessant
icings and drownings
had been self-absolved

                                              toward dawn
                                                stilled

somehow purified
by war

                                              unresponsive

until   years later
a majority of Senators
resurrected their
death

                                                  angel

How Many Will Be Too Many

fall

out the mouth

when

what should be

into arms

into bed

into money

into fortune

into future

instead

fall

surprised

spun around

twisted

with

or without words

with

or without explanation

warning

and are caught

on screen

by pavement

between states

fall

somewhere between

living

and dead

breath

caught

becoming shallow

rapid and then

fall

in our living-

rooms even

behind our closed

eyes repeatedly

fall

without indictment

with the hours

like clockwork

O, Sorority,

please turn down your music.
The loss of country
feels comprehensive
in these last throes of Jesus-
freak white conservatism.

Thousands of hogs drift
like bath toys in the plague waters
of the diminishing hurricane.

I want to tear up my money:
In God's Wind We Twist.

So maybe Bitcoin. But then
it seems somehow there would be
less of us, or more precisely

we would be converted
into a heaven of heat in the upper story
of a hangar-shaped server farm.

Come back, northern white rhino.

The mole in my basement
awaits better weather,
a more complete darkness.
All I can offer is the squeak
and groan of the washer/dryer.

Is that closer to love?
Is that closer to an honest
reckoning in the wilderness?

I don't know. What I do
know is that the sisters
are now dancing unironically
to "This Is America."

Neighborly

What I want to know
in the furling of summer
is how many flags
are too many flags?

Stars, however brightly
they shine—polyester—
overwhelmed by
the bloody bars.

Someone cracks a smile;
another cracks a beer.
It all has the Fourth
of July feel of joy
on the edge of violence.

Speedboat captains
gun their outboards,
slicing green
beauties in two.

Music.
Impatiens.

Coconut-smelling
and all a little rude.
Dogs off leash
or lurkers casting shadows
on the otherwise bronze bodies.

One pennant declares
All Lives Matter,

meaning no lives,
in particular.

But what sort of a nation did we
think we would be by now?

Parkland

It is June, and not everyone
graduates. Not everyone
tears off their gowns.
Not everyone races
into the hot mouth
of the night in a borrowed car.
Tonight, there is no curfew,
but not everyone laughs
and throws popcorn
through the movie before
sneaking into a doubleheader.
Not everyone goes
to the all-night diner.
Not everyone passes out,
blissed, on the drive home
next to the one they love,
for now, while the city
runs in a loop by their window.
Not everyone wakes
to the first pale flush
of morning on the houses
of their neighborhood.

Favor

Because my mother had to leave
to work at the hospital early,
I went, half-awake, to stay
with neighbors whose own kids
had grown and moved away,
which is how I became connoisseur
of basement rec rooms,
their overstuffed chairs
and untuned pianos,
crowded displays of photos
in second-best frames.
Here were the boys and girls
I wanted to befriend,
their likenesses captured
twenty years ago in this
very same house, or else
outside in the jonquils,
exactly where I would stand
to get the school bus
after I had watered
the neglected terrarium,
after I had banged out
a flat "Chopsticks" and watched
exactly two episodes
of *ThunderCats* and wondered
why I had been born
twenty years late and if
my mother was tending
to someone breathing
their first or last, just then,
and if living in such a green
world made one lonely
and if I could learn to love
that loneliness for itself.

Working Labor Day

Not so difficult as when
I finished driveways,
my hands in funk-
smelling, leather-palmed
gloves, the black,
acidic sealant flecking
and burning my shins
and calves.
                    Or up
a ladder, or in
a crawlspace
with white-faced hornets,
reaching for a rusted-shut
valve. Top 40 radio
keeping our minds off
hunger. Parallel
to all the work
I haven't done:

my aunt
cleaning houses,
lugging a vacuum
for thirty years
like a fourth child.

Men in prison jumpsuits
picking up trash.

This time around,
I am more fortunate than most:
inside a classroom,
reconstructing a poem
out of splintered air.

What does poetry accomplish?

You do the work
and honor what is done.

Recent Dispatch

i

Francis at the bottom of the Marianas
Trench. Cold. His hands curled

with remembered cigarettes. There was
once this thing called land, this thing

called air. And sometimes, ribbons
of smoke drifting straight upwards

to where frigate birds turned in a double
helix. Now just this null gone

static with the slow, steady sift
of calcium—powder of their hollow

bones no longer needed. He thinks
of the waste of his robes, the clutch

of begging voices there; now there are
no human voices, only feather-ended

tubeworms fluting and the ceaseless
discourse of whales at distances

impossible to discern. His brother,
he remembers, was a bureaucrat with

a drowning look. Women and children
were going down with the ship.

ii

Francis doesn't believe in sirens;
each monster he recalls is human.

Amen. Francis believes he is down here
for a reason. Something required

his attention: shy eels, for instance,
living in his hair. Or maybe just

a rushing silence that needed to be heard.
He hasn't shaved his beard in recent

millennia. The impossibility of steel
rather than a symbol of devotion.

Francis vaguely recalls the strength
of the sun, the length of a day.

The compassion fishermen showed
to the gulls, throwing them bycatch while

the whale-watch barker cinched a knot
of hunger. Some gales, some blue-greens

were left unsaid. Now, in the Trench,
jellyfish are a far cry from transparent.

iii

Francis swallows brine. His throat closes
up when he thinks of the clownfish

frisking with anemone. His mother
was cold as the Marianas, but there was

a certain butcher's daughter before
he took his orders. Strange. He'd almost

forgotten what touch was. And here
the water touches him all over.

A brittle starfish feels its way slowly
up Francis's left calf. Five zippers,

five long stitches come together
in a fine-beaked mouth. He's reminded

of migrations, but here, seasons
have no purchase. He is beginning

to think this is original time, the blink
in which he is painstakingly silted.

Sometimes, what comes down to him
has a barnacle, a little volcano whose plates

part, the branched tongue flicking out,
a quick skein into lightlessness. Hunger

fronds are the same everywhere. Ah,
hunger. And again, the butcher, the butcher's

daughter caught in the rainstorm,
striding over a puddle, and Francis's

face shining. The brief flush in the present
attracts heat vent bacteria. Where one

plate plunges, one plate mounts
the other, there is life.

iv

It is easy to love the cardinal, to make
oneself a perch, advantage.

It is more difficult to love
anglerfish, bioluminescent bait,

to make oneself a patient lair,
a spawning cave. Beauty less agreed

upon, less a state of mind than
a factor of perfect adaptation.

A drift of stinging cells. The body
must be a blank, must be a shade

antithetical to that which comes
as a relief. Pressure. Few degrees.

He believes firmly in firmament,
but he got here by following a plumb

line and when the line gave out
the logic of an unbroken trajectory.

He fell across the threshold of each
successive darkness. Yes, he'd say,

it felt like abandonment, but a no-less-
valuable truth. He feels like a child

with supermarket panic, or a latchkey
kid. Dawning is simple arithmetic.

v

The time he has left here is a fraction,
denominator unknown. In the movies,

they are always saying 'forever.'
In the texts, it is 'shalt' and 'shalt not.'

Francis rubs his brine-white face.
He suspects he is becoming a definite

gray area. Unreasonable to solve
for x. The plate gives another shrug.

The butcher's daughter was always
leading animals in by a kindness halter.

She knew about time remaining in one
respect and was, in others, largely

in the dark. It was appointed her
to help scrub the floor at end of day.

Pink smudge above one eyebrow
where she had passed the back

of her hand, the spot where just last
year, yesterday, one second ago,

something pelagic grazed Francis
where he stood waving and wavering,

as though he were an amphora glimpsed
through heat. Anchor or anchorite.

vi

Francis wonders where to from here.
No upwards, only onwards. Diameters

and outcroppings. He feels himself
driven against a reef. He is a wreck,

but also a reckoning. The cardinal,
the cardinal was a cheat, a scar.

Far above, a school of barracuda.
Silver and gills do exacting red work.

They are the sea's concerns, and Francis
is grateful arms far outstretched.

Never Been

Neighbors' faces lit by blue
screens.   Junkies? Angels?

I want to say the latter
although I've never heard

of sports bras in all the iconography
or miraculous accounts of folks being

saved for a larger purpose which I can
hardly imagine as I carry my daughter

who cannot sleep onto the dark porch and up
the sidewalk in my arms   my arms

which do this with numb customary strength
and if   if they are   they *are* angels

then the yellow slit of refrigerator light
must be the gates opening wide to take them

back to wherever it is that would leave us
bereft and I know the world will be different

when they are finally gone—the yew trees
outside their windows, for instance.

Same trees. Same trees, in different light.

Venus Crossing

Venus crosses the sun,
and I am out on the lawn
observing through milkcarton-
with-pinprick the planetary creep:
cataract time-lapse, a rare
phenomenon, although I am
wishing the whole time
that I had rinsed the carton
more thoroughly. Count this
as one more item in the long list
of that which cannot be
seen directly. As when
my friend loses his contact lens
in the pool and dives in after it.
His absence, his concentration
rise to surface. Break it. He is
essentially blind in one eye,
searching out a membrane.

And here is the miracle:
he finds it. The friend is dead,
the pool filled in. Is that a grain
moving slowly across the grain?
The neighbors come to watch,
take turns with the milkcarton
camera obscura. Apropos
of nothing, Venus crosses.

Aubade

Walden Pond
is closed to swimmers,
now—high levels
of fecal chloroform—
but that doesn't mean
we won't soon be
Transcending.

This one is for all
the button-savers.

Love, we were
made-for-tee-vee,
sunset in our
first words.

Ruined for each
other, post-
coital silences
riddled with the bark
of sea lions.

I commence to take
the trash out proper.
It's mine now,
all the rinds
cast-off.

I'm building
a monument to you,
the funk
of you I love.

And now it's hot
and raining. We seek
each other's seams,
grow less permanent still.

ACKNOWLEDGMENTS

Thank you to the editors of the following publications for including poems from *Mercies in the American Desert* in their pages: *American Poetry Review:* "Lineage"; *Bennington Review:* "How Many Will Be Too Many" and "Stock Ponds"; *Colorado Review:* "Private Booth" and "Still Life"; *Conduit:* "Meep Meep"; *Crazyhorse:* "Dream of *Zenyatta* Dancing"; *CutBank:* "Satellite"; *Denver Quarterly*: "[Darling]"; *Guernica:* "Night Vision"; *The Massachusetts Review:* "Pina"; *Memorious:* "Clean Slate"; *Michigan Quarterly Review:* "Venus Crossing"; *Mid-American Review:* "At the Mouth of the St. Lawrence," "Mercies in the American Desart," "That Other Life," and "Time of Asters"; *The New Yorker:* "African Grey"; *Ninth Letter:* "Idyll"; *Poetically Speaking* (Michigan Radio): "Bunyan" and "Shelter"; *Poetry Daily:* "Pina"; *Poetry Quarterly:* "Left in Charge of the Garden" and "Undergrowth"; *Posit:* "Old Marble Vast," "Shaft of Light," and "Where Once"; *Sou'wester:* "Espalier"; *Subtropics:* "Aquarium"; *Third Coast:* "Recent Dispatch" and "Sing"; *Tin House:* "Neighborly"; and *Tinderbox Poetry Journal:* "Never Been" and "Unlearning Object Permanence."

Thank you to the editorial and production team at LSU Press.

Thank you, Sara.